THE
HOLE IN THE
CODE

Simple and Easy Honest Taxation System

WILFRED DON

ARCHWAY
PUBLISHING

Archway Publishing books may be ordered through booksellers or by contacting:

Archway Publishing
1663 Liberty Drive
Bloomington, IN 47403
www.archwaypublishing.com
844-669-3957

ISBN: 978-1-6657-2374-9 (sc)
ISBN: 978-1-6657-2372-5 (hc)
ISBN: 978-1-6657-2373-2 (e)

Library of Congress Control Number: 2022908803

Print information available on the last page.

Archway Publishing rev. date: 07/02/2022

CONTENTS

CHAPTER ONE

THE GREATEST AMERICAN LIAR

IT WAS THE WORST OF times leading into the year 2020 from a poor man's perspective. Three years earlier, a new age of presidency had come in, along with a party concerned with only one thing: fooling the public by changing rules to benefit the rich, mostly at the expense of the middle class. Working Americans, who produce the wealth of our nation through sweat and dedication, were caught up in a system from which most cannot escape. The actual wealth created goes almost entirely to the upper 2 percent of the population and will not flow downward to any extent that might help the average American worker.

Our former president and his party had control of our banking system and have continued to manipulate the markets by lowering income taxes even further for corporations who already paid little, as the IRS schedules indicate on the next few pages. In addition, pressuring the Federal Reserve to keep lowering interest rates so they can keep the stock market rising to false heights will soon cause a collapse. Yes, there is a bubble developing in the housing industry, the tech stocks, construction businesses, and others that will soon come tumbling down. History is about to repeat itself the same way the e-commerce bubble popped in 2000.

Lowering corporate tax rates allowed the prices of equities to skyrocket over 15 percent on average across the board, while artificial lowering of interest rates has done the same. Neither method is more than a manipulation of the numbers rather than real economic growth. But what did you expect when the last administration's financial advisor was a stockbroker? Now, some will have to pay the price for coming adjustments.

The same financial advisor from the last administration also worked for Reagan's administration in the 1980s. Talk about history repeating itself. During the Reagan/ Bush era, which had the largest tax reduction act in history, three recessions—one every term—occurred. Millions lost their jobs, many corporations went under, and property values declined below their mortgage balances. The RTC was established to clean up and liquidate the mess. History is now about to perform the same antics because of actions of the TRUMP administration in the United States. Just a note to remind readers: Every Republican administration since President Roosevelt has produced a recession. However, no Democrat administration has produced a recession during the same time period. Time will tell if Honest Joe and his current Democrat administration will continue to avoid a recession during their term in the White House.

While our debt is rising at a faster rate than anyone can imagine, our trade deficit with other nations is rising even faster. Our national debt is $27 trillion, and each taxpayer has over $220,000 of this debt to service in the future. Actual federal spending in 2020 as of October 1, 2020, was over $7 trillion, exceeding the budget by $4 trillion. This is what a conservative president brought to the table. Our nation's debt to total GDP is over 140 percent, compared to 1980 when it was 35 percent. Interest on our national debt is running more than $1 billion per day, even with the lowest interest rates in current history. Total unfunded interest incurred by the USA is close to $4 trillion or over $15,000 per adult in America. Personal debt of our citizens is over $20 trillion, amounting to over $60,000 per citizen. Now consider that there are generally two types of people in the USA: those who borrow money and those at the top who lend money. Those who make their money off their labor and those who make their money off their capital. Student debt from loans is at $1.7 trillion and growing to over $40,000 per student. This future shows a runaway train heading for a cliff!

With the average credit card balance at over $6,000, most Americans are paying the minimum amount monthly and charging their maximum every month just to keep up with bills. Inflation is running over 6 percent in 2021, although it may soften to just 5 percent next year.

Now how do we stop going further into debt? You can't do it with only $1.5 trillion of personal income tax revenue coming in yearly. And you can't get far on only $174 billion of corporate income tax revenue coming in. Corporate income taxes are coming in at only around 10 percent of what citizens pay. Noncorporations, about twenty-four million taxpayers, are paying the largest load, and over eight million self-employed taxpayers are paying much less because they have the biggest advantage: tax loopholes and being self-employed or being incorporated and living through their corporations.

There are over twenty-four million government employees, over fifteen million union employees, and twelve million taxpayers working in manufacturing—all receiving W-2 wages. They make up part of the 116 million private sector jobs. Things must change to make our taxation system fair for everyone and not just corporations and the wealthiest 2 percent.

Our nation's GDP decreased to $17 trillion in the second quarter of 2020 from $19 trillion in just one quarter for many reasons. The largest reason was the uncontrolled COVID-19 pandemic, which could have been controlled with simple adherence to protective clothing and programs to prevent its rapid spread. In addition, our leaders shutting down the economy was a big mistake, but they were too proud to wear masks and failed to worry about their neighbors catching and spreading the disease. When your neighbor catches COVID, it's an epidemic; when everyone in the nation catches it, it's a pandemic. Now the problems go on as the unvaccinated continue spreading the virus to millions.

A young baby recently came down with COVID-19, which caused a blood clot in her lungs. Doctors are trying to prevent the clot from traveling to her brain with blood thinners and IVC filters to catch clots in her veins.

At the same time, the publicans are borrowing money and wasting it as fast as they can in the hope that some of those proceeds will circle back to line their pockets. Isn't it nice to spend money from other people's taxes without it coming out of their own pockets? These foxes figure out how to give taxpayers money in exchange for their votes to benefit themselves. Well, it's time to stop this system and come up with a better way to balance our budget, reward the hardworking Americans who deserve the benefits, and prevent the United States from being held hostage by the rich and famous.

PUBLIC CHARITY.

" When thou doest alms, let not thy left hand know what thy right hand doeth."

So what is this *hole* I am speaking of? You would have to agree that something is not right when a country as strong as the USA is going into debt at the speed of light. This black hole is sucking away at the tune of $20 billion per day. Then on the other side of that hole, the rich and famous are gathering up the bounty due to our unfair and unbalanced taxation system.

The *code* I am speaking of is the current Internal Revenue Code.

CHAPTER
TWO

A LOOK BACK IN TIME

AS FAR BACK AS SIX thousand years ago, and in ancient Egypt before there was written language, taxation existed. Taxation is necessary to provide for the welfare of a nation's inhabitants. Archeological digs in ancient tombs of Egypt have uncovered pendants with hieroglyphs that indicate the area of Egypt where the deceased lived. These stamps indicated that they had paid the taxes necessary in their region of Egypt. If one did not pay tribute to the kings, they were in big trouble.

The Bible also speaks of kings who issued ultimatums to their people that all the world they knew should be taxed. Taxation provided the means to pay for the armies that protected the tribes and inhabitants. It's most likely that the kings themselves and the priests and pharaohs of Egypt, along with the ruling class, paid no taxes.

"And it came to pass in those days, that there went out a decree from Caesar Augustus, that all the world should be taxed" (Luke 2:1 KJV).

The definition of *publican*, according to the *Merriam-Webster Dictionary* is "a Jewish tax collector for the ancient Romans, a collector of taxes or tribute."

So nothing has really changed, as the most powerful in the nation continue to put the taxation burden on the working class. If you read the Bible, you will find references to the publicans who were the elites of the society at that time, and they taxed the inhabitants of the land.

Publicans were despised Jews who collaborated with the

Roman Empire (wikipedia.org). No longer Jews but modern-day publicans now rule the country.

In current days, they've erected or maintained public barriers (the Trump wall), supplied armies overseas (the Bush wars), and collected taxes hidden as inflation without taxing themselves as they live off their capital. Unrecognized capital gains rather than wages is their game.

Unlike today, tax collectors two thousand years ago were regarded as the lowest of the low as they charged and collected taxes from the poorest, who represented most of society back then. The tax collectors were very politically motivated and kept large portions of taxes for themselves, while still contributing large amounts to the rulers. Today we call these *lobbyists,* who influence our lawmakers and leaders.

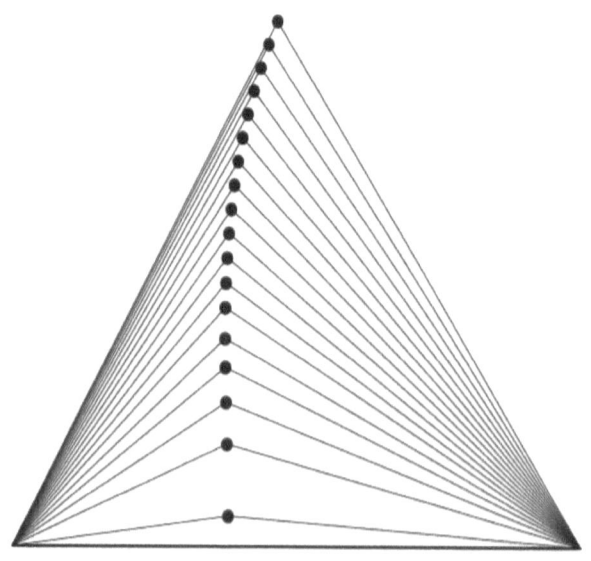

Pyramid Scheme to the Top. Big Money to Lobbyist, representing special interest

Each dot represents a special interest group. Lobbyists weigh heavily on determining tax laws and the flow of money, and power goes to congresspeople and senators and lawyers who write the laws that go to the president to create taxation laws.

In the beginning of time, taxes were paid to human-made gods by slaves, then to kings by the working classes, then to the landlords and chieftains. For thousands of years, gods, kings, priests, landlords, chieftains, and tax collectors received the benefits paid by the working classes. Now we are governed by the politicians. Laborers paid the way until the lowest classes overthrew their governments. Along with the invaders from foreign lands, the kings, priests, and tax collectors began paying tributes to a new ruling monarch. Eventually, after thousands of years, the workers rebelled, took over their governments, and began to tax all the people of their lands on some type of equitable basis. Today, we have lawyers and judges who write and dictate the taxation policies to benefit the rich and powerful and not the labor classes. Then our Congress buys into the laws that create loopholes for themselves, and they have the final vote after endorsement from the president.

CHAPTER
THREE

IMAGINE A BETTER ECONOMY

WHAT IF WE COULD COME up with a federal taxation system that would balance the budget and start to reduce our federal debt? Perhaps the new system could slow inflation so that average people don't have to see their savings depleted due to cost of living tripling every generation.

Wouldn't it be better to have less taxable income and a low cost of living, rather than the opposite? Paying more and more of your income back to the government because of progressive tax rates leads to less take-home pay. This leads to keeping less because the cost of living continues to rise monthly. This also causes reduced purchasing power for simple goods and services.

Let's see what the prices of a few items were when I was in grade school in the 1960s.

- postage stamp: three cents
- candy bar: five cents
- bottle of pop: ten cents
- loaf of bread: sixteen cents
- gallon of gas: twenty-seven cents
- average yearly income: $3,510
- new home: $7,300

Just a rough estimate shows us that in the last sixty years average prices have gone up a multiple of ten times, and this happens about every third generation. But now inflation is running about fifteen times that rate—except for new home prices, which have jumped almost 30 percent in just one year due to artificial lowering of interest rates by our government. At the end of the day, you are better off paying a lower cost for a home at higher interest rates rather than the opposite. If you don't believe me, just wait and see as the collapse in home pricing is coming.

The stock market will also soon make its decline, especially in tech stocks that are selling at high multiples of earnings. SPACs, Bitcoin, recent IPOs, and bonds will all decline as interest rates rise back to normal yields. The fat cats who created these will enjoy dwindling your cash down over the next years as they live off the reserves they built out of your money. The only thing they will pass on to you is capital losses that won't save you as much on your income taxes. Perhaps it's time to create your own cryptocurrency or Mary-Jane company.

If you are already rich, you would like this system, because you have it made. You've probably figured out by now, with your tax lawyers and accountants, how to pay little to no taxes by converting taxable ordinary income to lower-rate taxable capital gains and non-taxable dividends. Perhaps you have figured out how to write off everything you spend, including your costs of living, as business expenses. Maybe you've worked toward lowering your taxable income so you don't have to pay any income tax, like the former president bragged about. The president of the United States paid just $750 in income taxes for 2018 and 2019. In a recent homeowners' ruling in Florida the, former president was allowed to live on his resort as an employee tax free, thus not violating housing ordinances. Yes, corporations are doing it now and paying lower income tax rates on their bottom line than the average rates paid by most Americans.

Here's an example: Converting personal expenses to business expenses to reduce taxable income for self-employed people or business owners is great strategy. Living expenses are not deductible for a W-2 wage owner, but they seem to have been deductible for the former president of the United States. Bill Gates is now the largest farmer in America but has likely never even driven a tractor, planted seeds, or harvested crops.

Further on, I will be showing you the greatest tax breaks for investing in real estate, like apartments, commercial properties, farms, land, and single-residential housing. It takes some capital to get started, but you need to leverage as much as possible with low-interest mortgage rates against these properties.

I built an electric car model in the 6th grade in 1964 and presented it to my school in a demo as we maneuvered around the gym to everyone's amazement. EV motors have been around for a long, long time. Including that golf cart, you enjoyed while out on the course.

For example, let's look at Tesla, Inc. This company makes electric cars and batteries. Their stock has made certain shareholders billionaires because they pay little to no federal income taxes and have benefited from low-interest rates. Their stock now sells for over four hundred times earnings. Electric cars are not new. I drove an electric car over twenty years ago at a Las Vegas industrial show. It felt like driving a golf cart to me, and I was not interested. I thought the price was overvalued for what you got. Rockets to space are not new either. Many apes, dogs, and astronauts have been there and done that.

A deeper look into Tesla shows that the company has lost five billion dollars since its inception and has debt exceeding seven billion dollars.

(5,399,000) 2020

           (6,083,000) 2019

           (5,317,832) 2018

(4,974,299) 2017

The great thing for Tesla is that they can carryover the five-billion-dollar loss into the future and wipe out any taxable income they had in 2021.

An analysis of its numbers show it currently has a return on assets of 5 percent—less than my investment in high-yield bonds. Its return on capital is 7 percent, and it pays no dividends. But due to control of its stock by institutions and a group of elite investors, Tesla keeps is price at a ridiculous four hundred or more times earnings. This makes Elon Musk a paper billionaire. If it keeps daily paid blogs going and wild-eyed ideas cooking to the public, Elon Musk will hold on to his cult following. Along with the manipulation of the stock prices, they might hold the prices up to this level for longer than expected. In the last few years, Elon Musk has not paid much income tax due to his scheme of not paying himself much salary. When an executive does not pay himself a salary, he makes the bottom-line shine. The earnings per share shoot up and sometimes make the company appear profitable. The stock goes up in the market based on a multiple of the earnings per share. The result is the stock value of the executives goes up four hundred time—or more in the case of Tesla—making the tax-deferred stock value of the executive in the billions. This not only prevents any tax liability currently but defers the taxes until later at a lower capital gains rate when the stock is sold at multiples far more than the value of their salaries.

Soon Ford, GM, Rivian backed by Ford and Amazon, Apples new EV venture, Volkswagen, and many Chinese EV makers will catch up with Tesla, and then Tesla's stock will plummet. But fools are born every day and are attracted to anomaly, which keeps Tesla stock selling at magnificent multiples. What goes up will also come down in the stock market, as there is a loser for every winner. One lesson for self-employed businesses is to not pay yourself a salary, live through your company's debt, and expense everything through the company.

CHAPTER
FOUR

INTERNAL REVENUE SERVICE TAX CHARTS

Table 1. Tax Brackets and Rates, 2021

Rate	For Unmarried Individuals	For Married Individuals Filing Joint Returns	For Heads of Households
10%	$0 to $9,950	$0 to $19,900	$0 to $14,200
12%	$9,951 to $40,525	$19,901 to $81,050	$14,201 to $54,200
22%	$40,526 to $86,375	$81,051 to $172,750	$54,201 to $86,350
24%	$86,376 to $164,925	$172,751 to $329,850	$86,351 to $164,900
32%	$164,926 to $209,425	$329,851 to $418,850	$164,901 to $209,400
35%	$209,426 to $523,600	$418,851 to $628,300	$209,401 to $523,600
37%	$523,601 or more	$628,301 or more	$523,601 or more

Table 6. 2021 Capital Gains Brackets

	For Unmarried Individuals, Taxable Income Over	For Married Individuals Filing Joint Returns, Taxable Income Over
0%	$0	$0
15%	$40,400	$80,800
20%	$445,850	$501,600

Trusts & Estates

If Taxable Income Is Between:	The Tax Due Is:
$0 - $2,600	10% of taxable income
$2,601 - $9,450	$260 + 24% of the amount over $2,600
$9,451 - $12,950	$1,904 + 35% of the amount over $9,450
$12,951	$3,129 + 37% of the amount over $12,950

Now let's look at what corporations pay: 21 percent.

But the question is: 21 percent of what? Maybe nothing.

25-Mar-20

Corporate Tax Rate Schedule, 2020

For taxable income over	But not over	Tax rate is
$0	—	21%

Source: Internal Revenue Service. 2019 Instructions for Form 1120: U.S. Corporation Income Tax Return. January 2020.

It is obvious you want corporate tax rates and capital gains rather than personal income tax rates. You want to hold your wealth in corporations, equities, and real estate. You want to live off your borrowed money on your properties and try not to pay yourself ordinary income. You need to get out of cash as there is no return worthwhile on time deposits as they grow more slowly than inflation. For example: Some of richest men in America and the world—like Elon Musk—pay themselves little salary or ordinary income. Recently Musk moved into a modular home in South Texas in order to establish a homestead. However, he lives through his company where he writes off most of his living expenses.

This allows billionaires to pay the lowest taxes available in the system legally. They're living off their borrowed money while deducting the interest as a business expense on those borrowed monies. This produces capital gains that will be taxed at much lower rates in the future. It's reported that Elon Musk paid no taxes at all in two of the last ten years, but in other years he paid capital gains taxes when selling off his equities in the companies he runs. It's perfectly legal to make the holes in the tax code work for you, so you need to join the system. This will be your first move toward financial freedom.

Most corporations pay less than 5 percent on federal taxes on their gross income. Less than 1 percent of their gross income goes to local and state taxes. Meanwhile ordinary working-class people pay much higher rates, with some exceeding 37 percent of their adjusted gross income. Sure, the highly paid W-2 taxpayers' income is adjusted for certain items, like other taxes paid up to a ten-thousand-dollar max, medical costs exceeding

7.5 percent of their gross income's contributions limited to 50 percent of the AGI, and some miscellaneous minor job-related expenses. Mortgage interest is limited to only the amount on up to $750,000, which is very low considering the lowest mortgage rates in history. Or you can elect to take the standard deduction and not itemize. But why not have both? Let your businesses deduct all the medical, interest, taxes, and all other expenses, and take your standard deduction as well. Live in your own apartments, farms, and ranches like the ex-president, and reap the benefits.

What the publicans don't say is that individuals pay off the top line. Corporations pay off the bottom line. Get it?

A flat tax does not work, because the flat tax would benefit the wealthy even more. Do the math. The corporations would continue to pay a flat tax on the bottom line while hard-working American individuals would pay the top line.

CHAPTER
FIVE

TOP LINE VS BOTTOM LINE

MY BACKGROUND AS A CPA has given me a lot of insight into taxation, and I prepared over two thousand tax returns for wealthy individuals early in my career. Then I moved to being a CFO for large to medium companies and concerned myself with mostly corporate taxation. While I prepared taxes for wealthy individuals in my early career, I learned the advantages of being self-employed and the power of incorporation. Trusts, estates, and limited partnerships also avoid taxation on income and lower overall taxes to the lowest possible amount to benefit these organizations.

At the same time, I struggled for the first twenty-five years of my career and managed to live paycheck to paycheck and build a little net worth over that period. Then came the Reagan-Bush years, and Reagan had the first huge tax breaks with his caucus that controlled Congress at that time. I found out that all the equity I'd built in my home would soon disappear under the Reagan and Bush administration in their so-called trickle-down economy. Low interest rates, lower taxation, and inflation have a way of building a false economy and values in equities. Like what we are going through now and during the Trump administration, both slow down the economy. Society has more money on the bottom line, so there is less drive to make numbers. Society backs off when given these opportunities, like a rich kid lacking drive because he just inherited a fortune.

Currently, new homes sell for four hundred dollars a square foot on the average. A simple meal at a restaurant cost more for one person than what the Republican caucus wants to pay for hourly minimum wage. A simple light bulb costs over four dollars. A simple men's haircut is twenty-five dollars. Come on, people. Can't you see what's not right? All this is caused by inflation, while your government says that's not what's happening. Remember, the real numbers don't lie; the administration makes up the numbers that lie!

We are on a runaway train, all due to our fiscal policies. Our national debt, our unfair taxation system, and our banking system pumping trillions of dollars out are building a fake economy. Other nations are doing the same thing. But does one fool need to follow the other fool? Our currency today is fiat, like a Ponzi scheme that keeps printing money to cover payments that keep piling on.

These nations print money and then borrow more debt, and the costs trickle down to the taxpayers. The publicans always have a more secretive plan by borrowing money and then wasting it. They waste it on themselves, their friends, and their lobbyists. So, who wins and who loses in this political game? The retired, elderly, and poor lose, along with the middle class, as the rich get richer. Inflation eats away all those average citizens have worked for. Their retirement plans, their social security income, health benefits, savings, social programs, and any other fixed incomes are all diminished.

Ask yourself how today is different from seventy-five years ago. Both parents must work, just like mine did to make ends meet. In fact, in our family, my parents had two jobs: one as a schoolteacher, the other as an army officer of high rank. Both retired with pensions and benefits. Then they took on new vocations and worked another twenty years before retiring again. By sixty-five, they had two social security checks and two teacher pensions coming in, along with my dad's military retirement check. My mother continued to work for a private school, but my father was disabled due to complications of injuries sustained in World War II. I will say with all this, they were considered middle-class Americans, but they never got rich.

My father obtained enough schooling to have a doctorate and my mother received a college degree in education after they were forty years old. Even though they seemed very successful, they still never obtained what the *richest* of the rich Americans have been able to. That's because they were paid as W-2 employees, and they paid lots of taxes as a result.

CHAPTER
SIX

HOW THE GAME IS PLAYED

I WANT THE READERS OF this book to know that if you can't beat the system, you should join. We need to do this because the publicans won't change the taxation system to hurt themselves, and the internal revenue code will not be made simple. Why not? The code is so complex that only the best of the best tax experts understands and can interrupt it. This is done intentionally, just like the fine print on every signed document that most people never read or have time to understand.

Lawyers write them and citizens don't understand them, but we are all governed by those who write and interpret the laws in our courts.

LLCs, C Corps, S Corps, LLPs, and Self-Employment

The advantages of all these are tremendous. If you are not part of, the owner of, or a controlling shareholder in one of these, you are passing up on a large advantage you could have in America. Democracy works; it's just that you must figure out where all the ropes are to become a swinger in today's economy.

Can you really afford to continue working for a W-2? The fact is that cash is king! The golden rule in America is that the person with the gold makes the rules! Our current tax code benefits poor investments, tax cheaters, poor management, wild-haired ideas and illegal transactions.

No matter what business you select, you want to take Cash for your transactions because businesses that take cash have the option of not reporting it. Consider the mafia, thieves, gangsters, drug pushers, sex workers, and casinos. All these illegal actions pay little or nothing in taxes. We must change our system to make illegal transactions taxable in America. They are under the code but have little chance of enforcement, except in very few cases.

There are not enough IRS agents to handle the millions of tax evaders in the USA. For example, let's look at a large corporation called Amazon. Amazon, with their billion-dollar computer systems, has put millions of small businesses out of business. They are a cash business and take payment at the time orders are placed. They pay little in taxes and for many years paid no federal taxes at all. This led to lowering interest rates, along with the building of a monopoly in internet ordering for goods and services. They have so much cash flow that they must spend it on buying and starting other business unrelated to online purchases to be able to put their excess money somewhere that can make a good return on their investment. At the same time, until recently, Amazon could not pay the common worker even fifteen dollars an hour.

Getting back to cash businesses—it would be easy to set up a legitimate business on the surface but then launder money through it, much like our former president allegedly did before taking office. His casinos took in lots of cash, and then they could have paid for the family through skimming and laundering money through it. Ask yourself how a person lives high on the hog while paying little or no federal taxes. At the same time, they're showing losses in just about everything they run. How do they do this and then file bankruptcy multiple times, as our former president did?

International companies, tax havens, unrecorded transactions, you name it—the latest tax returns of our president indicated he paid consulting fees of twenty-six million, but to whom did he pay those fees? He paid over seventy thousand dollars for makeup and hairdos and over two hundred thousand dollars for photos. He transferred hundreds of thousands of dollars to family members without being taxed. I thought he was the best at everything and knew more than anyone about every subject, but his taxes indicate he can't make a profit. I will give him credit for knowing how to avoid paying federal taxes!

Bankruptcy is another way they steal from the American taxpayers, their vendors, and the government. The former president had over seventy million dollars of foreign income, with a lot coming from Turkey, as reported by the news networks, that was untraceable and undetectable. It isn't the right way and shouldn't be the American way.

And then the federal courts allow them to do it repeatedly over a set period, with no end to it during their lifetimes.

Personally, I do not condone this type of debauchery, and I do not believe in bankruptcy laws, except under certain conditions such as death, tragedy, acts of God, and total loss of income due to disability or continued illnesses of individuals.

I believe in a civilized society and proudly pay my taxes as an American citizen. Perhaps it's because my ancestry did not come from a Fascist or Communist country.

CHAPTER
SEVEN

LEGAL WAY TO LOWER YOUR INCOME TAX

BUT NOW LET US TURN to both legal and some illegal ways being allowed by our current federal tax code and why there is a hole in the code and its enforcement.

First, wage earners pay taxes on the top line, which is called the adjusted gross income. Businesses pay taxes on the bottom line, which is called taxable income after every conceivable item is written off.

My estimate is that 50 percent of all taxable income in the USA every year is not taxed! As our current president, Joe Biden, said last night on the news: These actors are tax cheats.

That's why proposals made by some in Congress calling for a flat tax are even more unfair. The only tax we should have is one on spending, called a consumption tax.

Businesses use the following methods to avoid taxation and delay payment of their fair share of taxes.

- Deferring income to another period
- Overdeclaring their liabilities
- Underdeclaring their inventory and personal assets, such as holdings of diamonds, gold, and other precious business properties
- Using a cash method of reporting instead of an accrual method
- Using a completion method of reporting receipts
- Capital gains and losses instead of ordinary income
- International income shifting and manipulation of allocations of expenses between countries

- Not reporting taxable income, and never filing a return
- Shell companies
- Hiding income in foreign offshore accounts— (For example, the former president set up hundreds of offshore corporations in Hong Kong during his administration.)
- Using taxpayer's election campaign funds for personal use
- Cryptocurrencies and nonreporting of gains
- Removing fixed assets and converting them to personal assets
- Hiding personal assets, like precious metals, cash, and jewels and physically passing them undetected to the next generation
- Deducting expenses that are not business related
- Purchasing of depreciable assets and taking accelerated write-offs.
- Accelerating deductions with (Sec 179) depreciation dump.
- Kickbacks, bribes, extortion, and blackmail
- Failing to match income with associated expenses during the same time period
- Speculating and hedging
- Running nonprofitable companies to launder money
- Shifting corporate income from country to country
- Conservational easements given to trusts for tax write-offs
- Simply not reporting income to the Internal Revenue Service

Why should a corporation be able to deduct losses from operations on ventures that will never be successful or just because of poor decision-making? Underneath the surface we find they are simply tax-avoidance schemes in some cases.

So why don't we put a stop to this madness that prevents America from being a great society instead of continuing to put our nation in debt further and further for the benefit of the top 2 percent?

CHAPTER
EIGHT

THE CODE WITH THE HOLE IN IT

ABOUT FORTY YEARS AGO, I graduated from a university in Texas. My first job out of school was preparing taxes, mostly for rich people.

I came up the ranks as a food preparer, paperboy, lawn keeper, US postal-system truck driver, bookkeeper, and then CPA. I worked for a small CPA firm in West Texas and prepared over two thousand tax returns during this tenure before leaving to work for the ninth-largest corporation in Texas at that time, in their tax department. Most CPA firms work mainly with self-employed individuals, corporations, small businesses, estates, trusts, foundations, nonprofit organizations, and so forth.

They do a lot of tax work, but they also audit, consult, and provide other business needs. I recommend you find a good one if you plan on being self-employed.

Personally, I enjoyed the work, but it was not challenging enough for me. I could not get ahead if I continued in that business. Sure, I would be considered middle class, but I could not save any money or build any net worth while working for a W-2.

Finally, after I turned forty, I had the chance to buy out a failing business owned by an international group during the Bush recession years that started me out in my own corporation and on the road to success as I had imagined it. As the chief financial officer (CFO), I had the inside track on this business and saw a great opportunity to turn it around.

That's how I have become a multi-millionaire, philanthropist, entrepreneur, real estate investor, and stock market investor. It's called the *hard way*. And I have paid millions upon millions of dollars toward both personal and corporate income taxes. This is how I did it.

- I took advantage of the power of incorporating.
- I took the advantage of being self-employed.
- I stopped working only for a W-2.

I have paid many millions of dollars of income taxes, property taxes, sales taxes, excise taxes, registration taxes, fuel taxes, and many more, and I've enjoyed paying my fair share through all these years. I see it a privilege to pay taxes, not a curse, and you should see the privilege as well. Income taxes are just a necessary and ordinary cost of doing business.

Let's discover some of the businesses and techniques used by millionaires to remain successful so they do not have to work for a W-2.

Land ownership for farming or just recreation or owning rental properties are hard businesses to get into unless you inherit the farm or other real estate. But after you have made your millions, you need to invest in land, commercial buildings, real estate, and rental units. You can see this in action, as Bill Gates is now the largest farmland owner in America. The advantages come in when you write off all expenses and then delay profits until later when you sell the assets at capital gains tax rates.

Farming and fishing are businesses with the greatest tax advantages on the face of the earth. As a tax preparer for many wealthy farmers, I could make tax returns show profit small enough to get them low-income tax rebates from the government or avoid taxation all together; it was their choice. Imagine that: a multi-millionaire landowner getting a low-income tax rebate because the code says they can. It's all done within the legal rules of the internal revenue code.

Deductions for farmers include:

- all the crops and livestock they can eat for their family,
- meals and entertainment (hunting, fishing),
- vehicles for the whole family,
- travel to exotic locations as long they attend a convention or look at another farm, and
- costs of growing crops they designate as their children's portions, making them appear self-employed.

In the Trump family, the children were given huge salaries, even when they were in high school.

But wait, that's not all. A few more benefits farmers can receive are:

- loans from the government for living expenses that are never paid back,

- government subsidy payments if they don't want to plant that year,
- government deficiency payments if they don't like the prices they got,
- forgiveness of their debt if they go into a government liquidation,
- government farm improvements for things like underground pipe construction,
- payments by the government to waste and destroy production (e.g., plowing under their crops or dumping their milk),
- not reporting farm government liquidation as a bankruptcy (therefore maintaining a good credit history and enabling them to get back and do the same thing again),
- not making estimated tax payments during the year, and
- waiting until the year is over to pay their tax liabilities (giving them time to manipulate their taxable income to their desired results).

I once knew a young farmer who was worth millions after his inheritances. He drew government loans for over twenty years, never paying back any principal or interest. He was then forgiven of those debts, which totaled over six hundred thousand dollars, in a method used by the Farmers Home Administration known as farmer insolvency. This allowed the farmer to avoid filing bankruptcy, which kept his record clean. During that time, he paid no income tax and just a little in social security tax—in twenty years. But he never missed an annual ski vacation along the way. Today he is an elected government official while his capital from his inheritances continues making him money.

Let me add that some hard-working immigrants with large families have done quite well starting with nothing and working hard on the farms. One tax client of mine who I worked with on getting a bank loan for some equipment to start his citizenship accumulated a twenty-five-million-dollar estate. When he passed on, he left his estate tax fee to his spouse and then on to their several children. Along the way he paid just thousands of dollars in income tax. And the Estate gets to revalue the deceased assets giving a stepped-up basis of the assets to market value. This method is available to every taxpayer at the time of death.

But this is an exception as these older farmers have been replaced by Billionaires and third and fourth generation farmers. Most don't hit a lick and spend more time looking for illegals to drive their tractors and do manual labor than doing the chores themselves. They were blessed not only with their grandparents' hard work, but also with the tax laws of the United States of America and government programs for farmers.

On the other hand, the farm laborers who worked for them got no free company vehicle. They did not get to split their W-2 with other family members or their kids. They did not get to travel to exotic places and deduct its expense. They did not get to deduct their food and lodging. They did not get to be forgiven of their debts after failing in business. They did not receive subsidies from the federal government related to their employment.

So why would they work for a W-2?

Get a business, work for 1099s, and enjoy the same benefits the rich and famous receive at any level of income.

Remember the tax code of the United States benefit those that have failed businesses—public corporations that never become profitable and pay no federal income tax and leisure businesses of the rich and famous. So, stick your neck out there and go in business for yourself. The government will hedge your losses to your benefit.

CHAPTER
NINE

TAX ME IF YOU CAN

LET THE GAMES BEGIN. ONCE you have made a name for yourself you can hire the best tax accountants and tax lawyers, so you'll have the best advice to eliminate your share of federal taxes. And it's all within the laws of the internal revenue code. I never thought it was a good method to become successful by eliminating federal income taxes.

Why pay for expenses you don't need just to eliminate paying income tax? You must pay out a dollar to gain less than one third back in lower taxes. It does not make sense. Truly, I believe most taxpayers just hate paying income taxes to their own country for various reasons. They are under the belief that they should not have pay taxes, but they sure believe in all the benefits that this government provides for them in the form of life, liberty, and protection of their families and properties.

Let's face up to facts. We can't beat the system right now; therefore, we must join in the system. Individual taxpayers—even lower middle class—must become self-employed or incorporate.

For example, if you are a janitor in a large city, you need to stop working for wages and hold yourself as self-employed. Double your hourly rate to your employer and become a 1099 contractor. If more than one will join in with you, consider becoming a shareholder in a corporation and divide the earnings at the end of the year after you run your expenses that were not deductible through the newly formed corporation. Get together with your shareholders and divide up the profits in some collective bargaining agreement. You will have more security by having more members to cover for you when in need.

You will, of course, need to consider some things. You will pay more social security taxes, but they are deductible from your gross income. Consider taking less out in wages to yourselves and have the company pay for most other expenses. Your goal is to move you down the tax brackets to the lowest available taxable income level.

You will be writing off like the big boys do when you start writing off things like snacks and breakfast and drinks. Large corporations have fridges full of good eats that are all written off as necessary office expenses, even though most would consider those meals and entertainment.

All your insurance for medical and dental, disability, most life insurance, and vision insurance costs are also included in what you can deduct. Corporations can write off the unpaid portions of all medical claims by structuring policies to pay all medical expenses for your employees and family. Let's go on vacation by finding a convention in the area concerning cleaning supplies or janitorial procedures. Your travel, hotels, amusements if included in the fees for the convention, and some meals if your hotel pays for breakfast, lunches, and dinners. I have not seen a corporation yet that excludes a portion of the hotel bill because it includes food and amusements. Remember, meals and entertainment are mostly nondeductible. Now you can buy that nice vehicle you wanted and perhaps one for the wife and children and consider them business vehicles. Just have the corporation purchase them, maintain and clean them, and of course pay for all the fuel.

To reduce your salaried employees, discuss becoming contracted employees with them. With a signed agreement, you have now reduced your payroll taxes on employees and charged them off as contract labor. (Our prior president does on a regular basis.) You will be asking your tax preparer to deduct his fees for his advice, services, and consultation. Also use accelerated depreciation on all the vehicles and equipment you buy in your business. This might include a home office deduction for an office in your home.

You will also be deducting clothing (uniforms) for doing your work. This would include clothing from your head to your shoes. Deduct laundry costs to clean them when needed and more employee benefit programs. In a recent ruling by the local government in Florida, where the former president now lives, considered him an essential employee, therefore allowing him to live—tax free—in his club house. I would bet he never pays for any meals, maid services, utilities, travel, or golf—for him or his family. Employee benefits programs in corporations can pay for many things. Medical bills, childcare on the premises, Doctors and nurses on the premises, travel, relocation expenses, hotels, entertainment, college classes, training abroad, and in some cases (like the Trumps) hairdos, clothing, nails, makeup, spas—you name it.) All of this is deductible in one or more of his establishments.

Borrow all your money, as interest is deductible too. Interest rates are at the lowest they've been in over sixty years. Take advantage of it. You might consider buying a storage warehouse to park, store, or just hang out in. You will now get things going enough to be able to pay for legal and accounting services, which all reduces your taxable income. All your office expenses will be deductible. You'll have no need to buy school supplies any longer. Offices, phones, cell phones, computers, laptops, and software are all deductible as business expenses with ownership of a corporation or simply as a proprietor. If you decide not to buy and rent, that will be a deductible business expense. You can also rent your vehicles, machinery, equipment, and other business properties. Never again will you not benefit from having to pay for repairs and maintenance as you'll run all these through your business and get a deduction for them. Supplies can include cleaning, toiletries, and other household goods you pick up at the grocery store. All taxes will be deductible as well. This includes sales taxes, tolls, property taxes, excise taxes, luxury taxes, and state income taxes and franchise taxes charged to your company.

Travel and meals now become important business expenses when you have your own business. Utilities would also be a major deduction and one you cannot deduct when employed by others. Do it right, and you can get all your utilities deducted, like our former president has been able to do it. Hire as many employees as you can afford to do your work for you as their expenses are fully deductible. This would include your children, spouse, relatives, friends and other family members. Then there is a category called other expenses that picks up everything else that corporations pay for that may be classified as unusual or perks.

For example: A Fortune 500 corporation that made blue jeans needed to keep their employees on the sewing machines to keep their clothes churning out without delay. They had a problem with women becoming pregnant and taking leaves of absence for up to year, so they installed a clinic on the facility for their ten thousand employees and dispensed birth control pills at no charge, along with other common drugstore items and prescription drugs to keep their employees on the job. They had a full-time licensed physician there on their payroll. Another doctor's office provided free daycare for their young parents on staff to prevent them being absent because of illness in their families. When there are seats available on their corporate jets, employees fill them without any documentation being done to tax them for their benefits.

Some of the newer tech companies install gyms, games, and playgrounds in their facilities for employees to use to save them on paying for outside services and just to keep their employees happy. Why can't you install the same in your business? Even pools and bowling alleys would not be out of the question.

So as you whittle down your taxable income, you lower your taxes to some of the lowest tax rates, as seen in the examples illustrated.

Here are some recent (June 2021) federal taxes rates paid by major companies that we all know. (Forget the 21 percent as it has little to nothing with tax rate, as these are their true tax rates.)

- Amazon: less than 1 percent
- Tesla: less than 1 percent (and zero since inception)
- DNOW: zero
- Google: less than 4 percent
- Apple: less than 4 percent
- Facebook: less than 5 percent
- Netflix: less than 2 percent
- GM: less than 2 percent
- Spotify: zero
- Ford Motor: zero
- Disney: less than 1 percent

Examples are given below of how publicly traded corporations keep control over their stock and therefore keep their stock prices up. Controlled ownership includes institutions, mutual funds, key employees and management. In the illustration, you can see that most of these corporations control the stock values by having groups of controlling interests. These corporations pay little in taxes and enjoy the current environment of low interest rates. Major banks are included in the controlling ownership that help these corporations remain a concern.

CHAPTER
TEN

SMOKE AND MIRRORS

MY OWN MEMOIRS ARE BEING shared with you so you can understand that the financial statements provided by public companies are simply management's best estimates of assets and profits, and they are not correct by any means. There are many accounting methods, cash, accrual, market value, GAAP, and financials adjusted for personal expenses. Public corporations are usually audited by independent CPA firms; however, in the past these firms, and even the big six in the USA, have been caught fudging the numbers. They are under pressure from top executives to manipulate the numbers for personal profits and concern over their jobs. For example, a New York Stock Exchange company I worked at for several years knew their depreciable fixed assets were worth only about 10 percent on the market and decided to sell them in a distress sale to be able to pay off bank debt that exceeded their net worth. Under GAAP rules and an audit by one of the big six, they were not required to write down depreciable assets back then to current market value. The next annual report to Wall Street showed they were solvent, but they were not. Their equity on the audited financial statements showed they had 180 million dollars of equity. About eighteen months later it was revealed that they were insolvent to the tune of fifty million dollars. Top executives had manipulated the numbers to hold share prices up. The charts show that most publicly held companies have controlled ownership that can change and manipulate share prices just as you'd control a puppet. The puppet in this scenario, though, is the uninformed general public. This NYSE company I worked for then showed the loss of the sale of their operations, which were due to the collapse of oil prices and a drop in drilling rig counts to almost zero. However, to keep from losing their jobs they withheld this information for over eighteen months. Then after paying down their debt to the bank, they were still far short. Bankers and top executives got together and decided to push the failure of the company to bond holders. They offered one hundred million dollars of 8.5 percent bonds to the public, who sucked them up quickly based upon misrepresented financials from a year earlier. The proceeds were then paid to the bank, who also benefited from the transaction. Later the true nature of the company was revealed to show that bondholders held unsecured bonds against an insolvent corporation. Soon the company defaulted on the interest payments. After legal actions, they offered the bondholders stock in the bankrupt company as the solution. Bondholders, not having any other resolution, accepted the offer and then lost their money later as the company sold out and left buyers with pennies on the dollar. They did, however, receive capital losses.

Another example hit me personally. I had just started playing in the market to see whether I could make some money in equities. After doing analysis of value companies on the market I came up with a company that had been in business for eighty years. Being a CPA, I analyzed their numbers and believed they were correct. But they were not correct *at all*, and that's when I found out the numbers don't lie—it's just that the top executives of companies lie about the numbers. So, when things add up properly, it means nothing! Companies have secrets they do not reveal. The first investment I made in CR Anthony stores was a total loss, which I found out after they filed Chapter 7. What amazed me was to find out the federal bankruptcy court said they had no assets. My unsecured claim was worthless. It seems all their inventory in their hundreds of stores were consigned. They owned no real estate. And the banks owned secured interests in everything else and would get preferential treatment. In the meantime, the officers all took off for other states far away from the mess and just left the court-assigned trustee to iron everything out. According to SEC rules and regulations for publicly held stock exchange companies, leaking inside information before the numbers come out is illegal. However, they are leaked intentionally to the related parties to help them profit off the numbers from good or bad news that will be announced in the next release. Currently the stockbrokers begin their pump-and-dump procedures. They know that stock prices will go down, so they try to sell off as many shares as possible, pushing off their equities to the unknowing public and group investors. Guys like me who worked hard for our money are misinformed intentionally to become their next victims. In the markets, there's always a winner and a loser in every stock transaction. If the stock goes up immediately after the sale, the buyer is the winner, and the seller is the loser. If the stock goes down, the seller is the winner, and the buyer is the loser. My second exposure to the Stock market is when I had 100.000.00 to invest and wanted a secure place to invest it. I called a local UBS office, and they visited to see if they could get my money invested in their firm. I asked for a stable investment with the great returns that were available at the time. They recommend a utility company.

I hate to admit it, but I took their advice line, hook, and sinker! They told me to invest in a utility company paying 8 percent dividends. Unbeknownst to me, they had inside information that the stock would drop the next day. They had information of its demise in the United Kingdom where their headquarters were, and they were about a day ahead of us in the market news. I was surprised to find out at the next quarterly news conference that they dropped their dividend altogether, making the stock drop in price by 75 percent. The brokers who sold me the sales pitch were under orders to pump and dump the stock immediately for the benefit of friends, employees, large investors, and themselves. It pays to have inside information, as you can see.

Perhaps it's who you know—even if they're crooks—rather than what you know that holds true. Today we have an even greater problem. Powerful people who are not directly involved on Wall Street manipulate stock values to benefit their friends, business associates, and themselves. They pump stocks to make them go up and do the opposite to make them go down. Just a small movement of, say, less than 5 percent can make millions of dollars in a day if you can get the timing down. One of these manipulators was our former president, who made market announcements during his last year in office to benefit his accompanying manipulators. For example, he could come out one Friday and say he is putting a tax on imports from a specific group of people. Immediately, the associated stocks drop. The short sellers with this information make millions. Then on Monday morning the next week he reverses the decision, making the stocks rally. The buyer group he works with make millions on the comeback in pricing. He manipulated oil and other commodity prices on a regular basis. He manipulated prices on other stocks by threats and intimidation. At the same time millions were dying of COVID-19 due to his arrogance. The USA only has four percent of the world's population, but America had 20 percent of the infections and 20 percent of the deaths from the virus during his tenure. All the while China controlled the virus, even though the outbreak occurred on their lands initially.

Elon Musk is the greatest manipulator of stock prices I have ever seen. He has a cult-type following to make Tesla hold a value of three hundred to four hundred times earnings. He is in the news daily, pumping his wild ideas that many take as gospel. Soon that stock will plummet. Ford, GM, and Volkswagen, along with many Chinese car manufacturers and already dominant Japanese car makers will eventually overtake Tesla in the electric vehicle market.

My point is that outsiders are now very powerful in influencing stock prices. These stock prices have very little to do with the real value of company's assets and profits. Take Dogecoin, for example, a coin-based pyramid scheme with little to no real assets at its foundation. If you are the developer or get in on the ground floor of these currencies, you might make a killing. Dogecoin, which started out as a joke, has gone from one cent to as high as sixty-six cents, only to fall back to today to around twenty-three cents a coin. But tomorrow, based upon only *hype*, it could go to a dollar. It's pure speculation, with odds worse than the poker tables in Las Vegas. As you can see, these coins can be manipulated greatly by the founders as they limit the number of coins to the market to drive up the pricing. Social media does the rest to drive up the prices. I am concerned that the entire stock market is being oversold in the same means. It's amazing what you can do to influence the public with paid social media blogs.

The average of stocks on Wall Street are now more than forty-five times earnings. Some tell us a correction is due, and others tell us we are near a disaster. However, controlling groups are holding prices since they have the majority shares. But then look at their amazing stock performances as price to earnings, and thousands of corporations pay nothing to Uncle Sam. Companies like Amazon, AMC, and more pay workers less than fifteen dollars an hour. In my own company I do not pay anyone less than twenty dollars an hour, and I provide full benefits.

It's no wonder the major shareholders of these companies are billionaires. Low interest rates and low taxes led to their stock prices going through the roof.

On top of that, the salaries these guys bring home is in the millions of dollars. Now look at the minimum wages they pay their W-2 employees.

I am sure the yachts these guys are building will be a deductible business expense as well. If they don't have a yacht, they have an island. I wonder who governs those islands, and are they out of the jurisdiction of the United States? Perhaps that's their new tax haven. If you cannot beat them, join them.

PRICE MULTIPLE TO EARNINGS 2021	PUBLIC OWNERSHIP % JULY 31 2021	CONTROLLING OWNERSHIP % JULY 31, 2021	TAX PAID as a percentage of Gross Income 2020	COMPANY SYMBOL
34	78	21	none	AMC overpriced
14	48	51	One percent	F
69	33	66	One percent	AMZ overpriced
7	8	91	One percent	VLKAF
400 +	42	57	One percent	TSLA overpriced
15	40	59	Five percent	BRK-B
28	48	52	Four percent	APPL
32	25	74	Five percent	FB
30	38	61	Four percent	GOOG
35	35	64	Six percent	MSFT
9	15	84	One percent	GM
55	21	78	Two percent	NFLIX overpriced
33	24	74	One percent	WMT

Electric cars are like all other electric items. They malfunction after several years and have to be thrown away or repaired frequently. A recent article in the news showed a Tesla replacement battery cost twenty-two thousand dollars. Recently, a crash of a Tesla in Texas killed the occupants, and the police reported there was no driver in the driver seat. How does an electric car catch on fire and burn to ground when it does not have any fuel on board? I have never owned an electrical device or battery-powered item (like a phone) that does not malfunction. Electric cars have over three thousand chips in them, whereas gasoline engines only have about three hundred. A lot are manufactured in China, and a lot will go wrong. I am not sure if Tesla is a Chinese, European, or American company since their chips come from China and over 30 percent of their cars are fully manufactured overseas. Recently, they had to recall thirty-six thousand vehicles for failing electronically controlled touchscreens.

Amazon is another anomaly. They consider the sales of billions of products by the millions of people selling through Amazon's site as their own. But in fact they are only acting as a broker for most the products being sold. They have put thousands upon thousands of small companies under in America with small downtowns drying up. Until recently they were paying the fulfillment center personnel less than fifteen dollars an hour. Their transportation services wear out our roads and highways, and they don't pay their due share of the costs of repairing them. At the same time, they pollute our air with their deliveries of goods and services. This has been made possible with the trifecta of low interest rates, low corporate taxes, and free internet services managed by billion-dollar computer systems.

Here are a tax havens all of us could enjoy.

- Bahamas
- Isle of Man
- Barbuda
- Hong Kong (where our former president set up corporations)
- Caribbean Islands
- Cayman Islands
- Countries allowing dual citizenship like Costa Rica
- Dubai
- Mauritius
- British Virgin Islands
- Anguilla
- Turks and Caicos
- Montserrat
- Guernsey
- Jersey
- Channel Islands
- Netherlands
- Switzerland
- Luxembourg
- Malta
- Monaco
- Singapore (40 percent of Fortune 500 companies operate here)

At least 366 companies in the Fortune 500 ratings have at least one company in a tax-haven country. At least six hundred billion dollars of taxes are avoided yearly due to companies having operations in tax havens.

Our government and Congress have put us in a state of hyperinflation, which gives the rich and powerful the best of both worlds. Our government is printing lots of money and distributing it to taxpayers in different forms to help stimulate our economy back to what is was pre-COVID. But it was a case of smoke and mirrors. Lowering corporate income taxes and lowering interest rates to zero was the goal of the previous president and his red army of followers.

Another note—in the past four years our country has been run by elder delinquents—older men who are totally out of their minds. I refer to them as the red army. It's obvious they tried to turn over our government and turn around our tax system to benefit themselves.

Just about everything they were working on turned into a total disaster. They even went to the extent of taking away Americans' votes at the ballot boxes as they attacked the Congress of the United States of America. Lowering interest rates caused hyperinflation for good and services. They gave money back to the rich by lowering taxes to the lowest rates seen in a century. What a screwed-up mess. Today we have little trust for our elected officials because of this red army and its leaders.

Citizens have always hated taxes. Paying your taxes takes away from your disposable income that you could have used to buy and enjoy things in America. For the last two thousand years, taxation has not been a popular subject, but it's a necessary one. What if we had a system that turned Americans back to loving their country? What if we had a system that does away with federal income taxes as we know them today?

CHAPTER
ELEVEN

TIME FOR A CHANGE

WHEN IS THE LAST TIME you hated the cashier at a restaurant when you paid sales taxes? How about the car dealer that charged you that huge 5 percent or more tax on your vehicle purchase? Do hotel taxes bother you when you check out of the fancy hotel in Las Vegas or New York City? I bet you didn't raise your voice when paying all the travel taxes associated with going to the Islands or other entertainment or just toll booths along the way.

Why? Because in your mind you felt like you got what you paid for, even though there may be 15 percent or more taxes added to the bill. Also, you paid it to friendly face rather than to a faceless government.

Paying as you go seems like a good system for state and local governments. Why not use the same system for federal income taxes?

Would you avoid paying those taxes and become a miser of sorts and not enjoy the pleasures of living in America? There might be a few people like that, but what would they gain?

They will save all their money and never spend it, enjoy nothing in life, and then die giving all they saved to their heirs. We all know inherited money is like lottery money and disappears very quickly after it gets in the hands of descendants who did not earn it.

So why not come up with a federal consumption tax? You pay around 5 percent every time you spend. All goods and services would be taxed. What would our national income be if 5 percent of the GNP of our country went to our treasury to pay for the national budget each year? Remember, half of all income is currently untaxed. But when the tax cheats spend it, it would be recovered. Not even the IRS's use of the Bensford Law can help find the tax cheats because the IRS audits the books as they are presented. They do not audit the assets that have been acquired off the books and outside the country.

With a national consumption tax, corporations would all pay 5 percent of every dollar they paid out. No one could avoid paying taxes—not even those made with illegal payments made under the table.

Think about the revenue it would generate without the angry hateful thoughts against our country. It works for states and local governments now. I have never seen a tax evader protest a state government for sales tax. Why? Because a third party collects the taxes rather than a taxpayer coming up with the amount of taxes he or she wants to pay every year.

Our government would begin to collect taxes from all the bad actors in America a little bit at a time as they spend their proceeds in whatever method they want.

We would hold the sellers responsible as independent third parties to collect and forward the taxes to the government. Harsh punishments and revoked business licenses would be the penalty if establishments steal and fail to return collected federal taxes. I can't imagine any business not wanting to remain operational and lose privileges.

When the gangsters, sex workers, and drug dealers use their illegal money, they will have to pay their share of federal taxes.

This seems like a fair way to collect taxes a little at a time and eliminate the hated tax return at the end of year, quarterly payments, and keeping up with all the records.

Payroll taxes need to stay in place, as this provides for Medicare and Social Security in the future when taxpayers retire.

This taxation system allows us to match tax revenues with spending and does not allow for all the loopholes used to avoid taxation or defer them into the future.

There will be no more capital gains, no more inheritance taxes, no more gift taxes, no more corporate or individual taxes. No more tax returns for estates, trusts, or nonprofits, and even partnerships—general or limited—would no longer report income and expenses.

There would be less paperwork, fewer headaches, and less hate toward our government. It would be a tremendous relief to not have to file tax returns any longer. Let's make things simple!

CHAPTER
TWELVE

THE NEW WORLD CURRENCY

IF YOU WANT TO BECOME a paper billionaire overnight, come up with your own cryptocurrency. Make up a billion digital coins for one cent each. Sell some to your relatives and friends for twenty bucks, as they won't disappoint you. The market value for your coins is immediately twenty dollars each. Congratulations! You are now worth twenty billion dollars.

Get your partners involved in a scheme to hold back most the crypto for themselves and drive the price up by having them sell their friends and families a few coins for thirty dollars a coin. The value of the coins just jumped to *thirty* billion dollars combined. Now it's time to pump and dump the coins on the market. With social media, you brag about how the price has gone from one cent up to thirty dollars a coin in such a short period of time. Hopefully your post goes viral, and the price of the coins continue to shoot up because of social media's psychotic frenzy. You also keep buying a few coins for yourself along the way at the next higher price daily to lead the market upward. When you need to cash out, sell a few coins for millions, and enjoy your new lifestyle.

Cryptocurrencies are 90 percent fraud, hype, and a lot of noise. Be careful gambling with cryptocurrencies. They're a blend of the old chain letter and pyramid schemes and seem to be working quite well for the founders. Of course, for every winner there is a loser of the same magnitude. The secret is to get in on the ground floor.

Let's face it. Paper money and coins are on the way out. Everyone will be paying digitally in about the next ten years. With a new federal consumption tax, it will not make a difference if you try to hide income from the government. Who cares if you have billions in hidden places? If you never spend it, you never receive goods and services. All you have is a sense of security and bragging rights. At the end of three generations, it will become someone else's money unless you can figure out how to take it with you. In the new digital age, the government will find it impossible to keep up with unreported taxable income and will audit all the transactions of the digital world.

My advice to all who read this book is to stop working for someone else. Become your own entrepreneur. Join the club like the wealthy do and hire some professionals to set you up properly. Then you will be able to deduct the list below and live through your company like the big boys do. These deductions can be yours, as you will be taxed on the adjusted bottom line rather than being taxed on the adjusted gross income you're currently taxed on. Included below are many deductions you don't get now. And if your ego is big, you can include gold-covered toilet seats like the former president of the United States. The limit to deductions has not yet been determined by the IRS. Corporations are now deducting rocket launches to the moon as business expenses. Jet flights into space, electric vehicles, yachts, bad business decisions, fake cryptocurrencies—all these buy excitement for the people who receive them, but are not taxed for the benefits they received. All these seem to be hobbies rather than productive businesses. But what the heck? If you can't beat them, join them until we come up with an honest and fair taxation system in the United States. These deductions can be yours if you are self-employed or own and control corporations.

Vehicles
Planes
Insurances
Meals
Travel
Entertainment
Life insurance
Clothing
Drug Store items
Medicines
Doctors
Child's education
College tuitions
Boats
Repairs
Office expenses
Parties
Supplies
Sundries
Wages
Sports
Banquets
Artwork
Rents
Donations
Advertising
Computers
Security
Internet
Social networks

It's time you get taxed on your bottom line and not your top line for just about every occupation. All should become self-employed, preferably through incorporation.

If you want to be happy for an hour, have a cup of coffee with friends. If you want to be happy for a week, get a puppy. If you want to be happy for a month, get married. But if you want to stay happy for a lifetime then become self-employed, incorporate yourself, and enjoy the same lifestyle as the rich and famous. Until the United States comes up with a fair and honest taxation system based upon a federal sales tax on consumption, we will never have a good taxation system.

REFERENCES

Britanica; Publicans definition.

The Holy Bible .

Yahoo Finance publications of Balance Sheet of Tesla and other Companies

Usdebtclock.com

NOTES

Publicans: Latin Publicanus, plural Publicani, ancient Roman public contractor, who erected or maintained public buildings, supplied armies overseas, or collected certain taxes particularly those supplying fluctuating amounts of revenue to the ruling state.

Retained Earnings which is accumulated losses of TESLA: Company has never made a profit since inception: shown are negative accumulated earnings by year: US dollars.

-5,399,000	2020
-6,083,000	2019
-5,317,832	2018
-4,974,299	2017

www.ingramcontent.com/pod-product-compliance
Lightning Source LLC
Chambersburg PA
CBHW021448210526
45463CB00002B/678